38 YEARS LATER

ROBBERY KIDNAP

EAST OAKLAND TIMES, LLC

EAST
OAKLAND

"The way I see it, if you want the rainbow, you gotta put up with the rain."

Dolly Parton

MY CRIME SERIES - BOOK FIVE - 38 YEARS LATER

Welcome to San Quentin State Prison! Come and meet your new "celly." His name is Brian and he is a hard worker with a penchant for veering off the well worn road of the 9-5. He has a story to tell about the potential hardships of taking a plea, living a full life behind bars, and the ways and manners of a young man who couldn't keep his hand out of the cookie jar.

Welcome into your understanding the man next door who ended up spending 38 years to life in prison.

The books of the My Crime series are neither meant to justify nor condemn the inmates on whom they are written. Rather, the books of the My Crime series propose to candidly communicate the upbringing, life experience, thoughts, and motivations of the incarcerated.

The My Crime series puts you as the judge. Your judgment will not simply be about the individual on whom a book is written, but your judgment will weigh the life circumstances that shaped his or her criminal disposition. The My Crime series takes the unknown inmate and presents his or her life for public evaluation.

Each book in the My Crime series is written on an inmate, by an inmate. Each book will progress from the Subject's childhood up through the commitment offense that brought about the Subject's current felony incarceration. Each book, therefore, will offer the big picture of the Subject's criminality as dictated to and written by a fellow inmate.

The My Crime series books are intended to fit into the present-day dialog on crime and punishment. As citizens of today's American democracy, the understanding we each have of right and wrong is the essential knowledge we use in taking political positions. Ideally, the justice issued by legislators and interpreted by courts is a justice that agrees with most citizens. If citizens agree with the justice being issued by the government, citizens will promote that justice as truth for the times.

As a society, we do not know ourselves enough to have the right answers on justice.

The My Crime series grants you the opportunity to sit and listen to the unknown felon and learn, as if you were on the bottom bunk, about your neighbor and what brought him or her to getting locked up.

Thank you for purchasing the fifth book in the My Crime series.

Encourage others to read the books in the My Crime series by leaving a review.

I welcome you to visit the webpage dedicated to this series to access additional content for this book and other books in the My Crime series. **Additional content includes phone**

interviews, book drafts, and supplemental offerings:

WWW.CRIMEBIOS.COM

Finally, I welcome you to read the last page of this book for information about the producer and publisher of the My Crime series, the East Oakland Times, LLC.

In liberty,

Tio MacDonald
Chief Editor

1

UPBRINGING

P eople take much in life for granted. Usually, we overlook the simplest of things: the smell of fresh cut grass, a home-cooked meal, the comfort a dog can bring, relaxing at a beach and hearing the ocean roar.

Life's simple pleasures are what I gave away. What do I mean by that? I am the only person in my family that has been to prison. I cannot attribute it to my upbringing. My older sister had a small run-in with the law due to check and credit card fraud. She ended up with probation. My life surely wasn't predestined to be this way, locked up for generations. Often, I look back, in reflection, to understand how my life took this turn. My Name is Brian Shipp and I and currently incarcerated at San Quentin State Prison for the crime of kidnap robbery. I am in my 38th year of a 7-to-life sentence. This is the story of how I got here.

I was born in Alameda California in 1958 to a loving mother and father. Alameda was a Navy town off the San Francisco Bay. We lived in a charming three-bedroom home. The home had a large backyard and a fireplace. It was a different world back then. The country had wrapped up the conflict in Korea. There were beginning talks of "make love, not war."

My dad worked as a barber. He was very good at his craft. Many of his customers had been coming back to him since the day he set up his chair. My mom was the typical housewife. Her daily tasks were to cook meals and keep the house clean. Despite the help that women gave us in WWII, the notion of women working seemed still a futuristic thought. It was uncommon for women to get equal pay as men back then.

My older sister and brother are four and eight years apart from me. When I look back at that time of my life, we were very close. I can't remember any fights we had back then. I could go to anyone in my family and ask for almost anything. Most of my childhood was blessed. I was happy and had plenty of friends.

✖ ✖ ✖

At my age of four, we moved 25 miles inland to Alamo California. The move marked the first significant shift in our way of life. My dad had always talked about opening his own shop. He could make a lot more money if he didn't have to pay a percentage to a barbershop owner for renting a barber chair. As a result, my dad bought his own shop where he set up business. It was his way of being independent and not work in someone else's barber shop. He wanted the American dream and to provide for his family.

Business was a little slow as he started off. Most of his customers were back in Alameda. It took a lot of word of mouth to actually get him out of the red and into the green. The new business was a highly stressful enterprise.

I guess the new stress took its toll on my mother and father's relationship. Shortly afterward they separated. While my parents were separated, my siblings and I tried to carry on as usual. It has never truly dawned on me the impact their marital problems probably had on my life.

My parents lived in separate homes. I assume they hoped to rekindle their love but sometimes when people separate they understand just how far apart they are. Couples often find that both may love the other, but they both want different things in life. My parents divorced a few months later. Their divorce was a shock to me. I was under the impression that they were just fighting and would soon make up.

Next came the decision of whether they should split the kids up or let us remain together. I guess they figured they would give us the choice. All of us siblings elected to stay with our mom. This may have been because dad was the disciplinarian. He was also usually gone when we came home from school. Mom was the voice of care and regard.

We spent weekends with our dad. He also would come by and pick us all up on Monday after we got home from school. Being able to see him on Mondays was special. He would take us to his apartment. It was a small one bedroom but cozy apartment. There we all had chores to do. He never used to do any chores as he would make reference to chores as women's work, so we cleaned. Us kids made his apartment immaculate.

My dad's friends seemed to warm up to us quickly also. Some of the persons that would come by my dad's were family members, distant aunts, uncles, and cousins. We would go to Shasta Lake with my dad and his friends. Most of the people that went to Shasta Lake went to party. I'm not saying my dad's intentions weren't to party, but he welcomed and watched over us. Our stay was usually a week long. It was a great vacation. We would ski and hike and sit around bonfires at night. We made smores before they were a household name.

The vacation would come to an end quickly. My dad would take us back to mom's place. I could see her smile as we pulled up. Then I guess a thought would overtake her and she would look at the ground as we exited the car. My dad would wait just long enough for us to close the doors to the car. With a short wave, he would drive away. At my mom's we sat around and watched TV.

My sister had an estranged relationship with our dad. They seemed to fight all the time. Maybe it was his way of parenting or his way of showing love. My mom really only wanted us to be happy and have fun with our lives. I think it was a phase that my sister and dad were going through. Nothing outrageous, just the typical father and daughter bickering. Nevertheless, their fighting would upset me because I wanted all of my family to get along. Despite me being the youngest, I felt as if I were the nucleus for harmony in the household.

My brother and I have an eight-year age difference. I looked up to him and was basically his shadow. He really didn't like when I would tag along with him. When I would bring up to mom my brother's resistance, she would tell him to take me with him. Most of the times we fought about that. If we weren't fighting, he would stick his finger in front of me and tell me to bite it. I would do so and he would thump me until I let go.

One time my brother woke me up in the middle of the night and told me to hurry and get ready for school. I got dressed as quickly as I could and ran outside. It was pitch black. He locked the door and would not let me back in. Nothing to intentionally hurt me, just annoying. He found ways to agitate me for his amusement. By doing so, I think he had hopes of me not following him around. Despite these types of conflicts, I still got along well with all of my family.

✖ ✖ ✖

I don't think my mom anticipated the great struggles of being a single parent nor the cost associated with being a single parent. Mom did the best she could to provide for and raise us. We lived like nomads moving between dwellings in Alamo and Danville, California. We had a limited income coming in. My mom worked as a waitress in various diners. She also received money from child support paid by my dad. Much of the diner work was temporary or at least felt like it to me. The sad part was that bills didn't wait for her to get another job. She eventually filed for welfare and food stamps. We couldn't make it without assistance.

All of the places we lived in were dilapidated. If the houses had back and front yards, the yards were full of weeds. Weeds left little or no spaces for me to play. The weeds could be as tall as me. Sometimes, there were holes in the walls from the punches or kicks of former occupants. I guess the property owner never cared to repair them before re-renting the places. I pretty much accepted the fact that these were the type of living quarters that mom could afford at the time. My main concern was having fun. I tried to accomplish that with as little parental supervision as possible. Mom wasn't a disciplinarian. She would only inflict her wrath if we disrespected her or each other.

Despite our financial straits, I was still relatively happy. I actually enjoyed growing up in various neighborhoods. I was outgoing and made friends quickly. Older people seemed to warm up to me and enjoy my company. If I was a bother to them, they never let me know. I held in my mind a belief that adults hold a fountain of knowledge. I would ask questions about any and everything to pick their brains. Nevertheless, it seemed as soon as I settled in my mom had plans to move again.

My mom started dating. She was an attractive woman and would be good for any man. She met a guy named Jack. They started seeing each other on a regular basis. I guess they both felt the relationship was going in the right direction, so we all moved in together. We moved to a bigger home in a town 30 miles north of Danville called Pittsburgh. The home was beautiful and had a yard full of green grass. We would play slip-in-slide on hot days in the backyard.

I can remember coming home one day and my mom had a smile on her face as big as Texas. She announced to everyone that we would have an addition to the family. She was pregnant. Jack seemed genuinely happy also. We all liked Jack. He would take us out shopping and buy us any toy we wanted. He kept us in new clothes for school or church. He had a convertible car. None of us had ridden in one before. He would let the top down and we would drive everywhere and let the sun warm our faces and the wind whip through our hair. Our favorite place to go on warm nights was Baskin-N-Robbins. I loved their ice cream. Jack would also take us to the Santa Cruz Boardwalk. He would pay for us to go on all the rides there. Our days would end with swimming in the Pacific Ocean.

I was enrolled in a new school. I didn't know anyone in the town or at the school but I didn't let it bother me. I was a likable person and people warmed up to me quickly. I was getting used to starting over. All schools seemed to have the same curriculum, so each time I started over I fell right in and wasn't left behind. I had a passion for math and music; I was a natural at both.

✖ ✖ ✖

W hen I was around 10 years old, I got a job working for the United California Bank. The work consisted mostly of cleaning up the parking lot and maintaining the foliage. At least once a week I pulled the weeds in the parking lot. I also trimmed the hedges. I loved the smell of fresh juniper when I cut it. I used the money to open a checking and savings account at the bank. The savings account would grow with each paycheck. In addition to the landscape maintenance job at the bank, I created flyers advertising lawn care for families that were on vacation. The slogan on all the flyers was, "Your lawn and plants will be greener and healthier when you come back from your two-week vacation!"

I was 12 years old the first time I bought my parents and siblings Christmas presents. It felt good and I continued to do so every year. This was done regardless of whether I had a lot or little money. I made sure everyone in the family had a Christmas gift.

I started playing the drums around 10 years of age. I wanted to be just like Mikey Dolan of the popular band, "The Monkeys." My friends and I played at the 6th-grade graduation. The performance was in the auditorium at the school. We were a hit. All the girls were screaming and yelling. I played a drum solo at the end. It was a song from Iron Butterfly called, "In-A-Gadda-Da-Vida." The crowd went wild. I really felt like a superstar. I was very popular in elementary school and paired up with the prettiest girl.

In the 7th grade I excelled in school. I took advanced Algebra classes. I also grasped Geometry and statistics. I enjoyed math. It was a great time of life. I was nominated for best dressed and finished in second place. These sorts of accomplishments made my parents proud of me. Despite of all the good I was doing, I also had a dark side.

CRIMINAL THINKING

My first misdeeds were relatively small. I began shoplifting in local stores. My first impulse to do so was around the age of 10. I took things that we needed at home from the grocery store or the local Five & Dime. I felt an immense rush from shoplifting. There was a great thrill experienced each time I walked out of a store unnoticed.

Once, I got caught stealing from the the local Gemco department store. The security staff snatched me up while I exited. They banned me from that store, which, honestly, wasn't enough of a deterrent for me against future stealing. I continued to shoplift, but I did not do so day in and day out. I changed my tactics into a new scheme. I would switch the price tag on an item in the store and then pay for it. Basically, I would find expensive brands and then switch the price tags with cheaper brands. I would then go to male cashiers because most men weren't familiar with the items. Later in life, I pulled the same scheme in automotive stores. In automotive stores, I would go the female cashiers as most of the women cashiers knew less about car parts. Not once did I ever have a problem or any suspicions from the stores and I did this on many occasions. Nonetheless, it wasn't enough. My idiotic criminal thinking would talk me into greater misdeeds. My head always had me thinking the grass greener on the other side, that a quick score would put me ahead. I was adamant against the poverty mind frame: in other words, accepting a life without what others had. I smoked my first joint around this time as well.

My criminality evolved into the burglary game. A friend and I broke into homes. First, I would knock on the door and hide, similar to the door knock game kids play. When we were sure no one was home, my friend and I would go around to the backyard and look through the windows. We preferred homes with doggy doors as the doggy door gave us a means for easy entry. On my belly, I was just small enough to crawl in a house through the doggy door flap. My friend would hold up my legs so I could fit in. Once inside I crept around the house to make sure no one was present. My heart would beat a mile a minute. I would then go to the back door and let my buddy in. We wouldn't ransack the house. All we took was food and alcohol. I never took any valuables, such as jewelry. We did this three times in three different homes.

My buddies and I would also take cars on joyrides. People often would keep their extra keys either balanced on the visor or under the floor mat. The first car we stole was a Fiat 850 Spider. We drove the car to the Cow Palace Arena in Daly City for a New Year's Eve concert. We were both 13 at the time.

7TH GRADE

In the 7th grade, my vision took a turn for the worse. I began wearing glasses. Also, my dad required me to wear dress clothes. My teeth were crooked and I wore braces. I was no longer the cute kid. I was now a weird looking glasses and braces monster. To add insult to injury, I had wild crazy hair. I became a type of outcast. I pulled away from the friends I had. I started spending most of my weekends with my older sister. She married when she was 16 years old. In those days, it was more common to marry that young. She's four years older than me. It was cool hanging out with my sister and her friends. My brother-in-law kept my mind occupied as well. He got me started helping him work on low-rider cars. We would often go to the junkyard looking for used parts we could salvage. It was a lot cheaper than going to the store to purchase them.

My brother-in-law and his friends didn't care what I looked like. There were welcoming of me for I was a curious and fun kid who was always ready to help out or join in on an adventure. Since those days, I have had a passion for cars.

4

COMING OF AGE

I value all my friendships and have always been a devoted friend. I'm a genuine person and would give myself or money to help others. If we were going somewhere, I would pay their way to help them enjoy the occasion. I have always been a good listener. My heart nor my character has ever been out to deceive or cheat a friend. I would go out of my way to be there; this is just what friends do. I honestly enjoy the act of giving. People would classify me as shy at first, but when they got to know me, they would be attracted to my heart and character.

✖ ✖ ✖

I was without a peer group and wanted to be accepted. I grew my hair long and stopped wearing the dress clothes my dad bought me. I began buying my own clothes. By purchasing my own clothes, my dad couldn't tell me what to wear. My attire was jeans and hiking boots. I also wore long sleeve Pendleton shirts, even on hot days.

Due to boredom and being shy, I experimented with drugs. I

used drugs to take the edge off and for conversation. At that time, I wasn't addicted.

One of my connections for psychedelic mushrooms, "shrooms," was considered a "Dead Head." He and his friends loved the Grateful Dead and went to every concert that was performed in the Bay area. After hanging out with them for a while, I found new acceptance. My new friends and I would go on hikes up mountainsides. We would camp out on weekends and smoke weed. A number of us played instruments. One guy played the bagpipes and my best friend played guitar. We would sit around campfires singing along like we were a commune. The pretty dead head girls and dudes all got along well. They all hooked up except me. I was liked for my personality. At the time, I was a follower of these friends. Before I was a leader. It was an ugly stage of my life.

✖ ✖ ✖

I got my driver's license and purchased my first car. It was a 1966 Pontiac Bonneville that I quickly turned into a low rider. I was the only guy in my high school with a low rider. I used to get a lot of attention when I pulled up. Interestingly enough, at school, there was also a lady with a low rider.

Daily, I would spend hours working on my Pontiac. My brother-in-law's cars were my inspiration. I needed stylish tires and rims and a booming stereo.

The great thing about my Bonneville was that it was large enough to carry all my friends. We would all pile in and go to keggers or house parties. I never tried to race my car.

✖ ✖ ✖

I, like most teens, rebelled against any and everybody. I had quarrels with all of my teachers. My woodshop teacher was cool, though not tolerant of weed. One day, I smoked a joint before going to class. He asked for my assistance with grading papers. I didn't think twice about going into his closed office and grading papers. When he walked in, he frowned. I looked up with a confused look on my face, trying to gauge his feelings. He said, "Learn to wear cologne. You reek of weed." I gave him a look as if I didn't know what he was talking about. He then added, "You'll ruin your life smoking that crap." I respected this teacher and wanted to listen, but as I said, I was in my rebellion stage and let his words of wisdom drift in one ear and out the other.

At age sixteen, I got a job as busboy in a local hotel. I have always been a diligent worker, so I quickly worked my way up to the title of lead man. The lead man position brought more steady work and longer hours. I worked overtime as much as possible. I wanted more money. I also sold lids of weed at school to earn money. A lid was the term used for an ounce. I would throw smoke out parties. People would buy my product and have a good time. Selling pot helped my income.

Selling weed was a lot easier to do at parties that the jocks threw. You would think that jocks would be clean and sober. Quite the contrary. Jocks were my best customers. A lid of weed cost fifteen dollars. Selling weed was a good income supplement. I was making around an extra $30 a day selling lids.

One day while standing in front of an apartment complex waiting for a customer the cops swarmed on me. I had four lids of weed, which amounted to a quarter pound. I didn't have time to hide it or stash it. They patted me down and found the pot. I was taken downtown to the police station. Since I was a minor, they called my dad. He came and I was released into his custody. They gave me a $200 fine to pay. Since it was under a pound, I received a misdemeanor. I was put on restriction for a month. Restriction was like a prison to me. I was used to being outside working and having fun, but now I was stuck in the house all day. I didn't feel like the punishment was just. I was seventeen years old.

✗ ✗ ✗

I found my first love during my senior year at Del Valle high school in Walnut Creek, California. Our classes were next to each other, so I would see her in the halls. Although I lacked the gift of gab, I ended up sparking a conversation with her. We hit it off immediately. It was as if I knew this woman my whole life. We could talk about anything and everything. Our shared interests brought us closer together. We were both athletes and loved the outdoors. However, when we talked about family, we were opposites. Her family was wealthy and offered her support in whatever she did. My broken home saddened her and made her feel empathetic towards me.

As our relationship progressed I proposed to her and she accepted. We were engaged. Things seemed perfect, but we lacked maturity. Plus, this beautiful woman loved attention. She would flirt with people all the time. Sometimes even in front of me. I didn't believe myself to be smart or handsome enough to possess such a beautiful woman, which led to me being jealous of her and her flirtatious ways. Eventually, we separated.

✗ ✗ ✗

I was feeling down and out. I needed to do something to take my mind off of my ex-girlfriend. My friends and I decided to throw a kegger. My dad was away on vacation. He left me in charge of the house. We had a huge party. Everyone that was anyone was there. I don't know how they found out, but kids from all over Contra Costa county showed up. Music echoed throughout the house and beer flowed like water. Everyone had a great time, drinking and dancing. There were many pretty ladies. I brought cocaine. Lines were shared. I felt like a celebrity. The party was a hit. I had another kegger party when my dad went on his second vacation.

✖ ✖ ✖

Those were great and spontaneous days. I tried black beauties and cross tops, types of amphetamines, when I wanted to stay awake. I also tried acid hits in different forms but never really enjoyed the high.

I remember my first acid trip. I was at a party at a friend's house. Everyone there was on it. These guys were messing with a girl who was really high. She was having a bad trip. Somehow, she managed to climb up a tree and was stuck. She was scared and kept calling for me to get her down. I was frying so hard I couldn't move to help her. All I could do was watch. I never felt so helpless. I knew that drug wasn't for me.

INDEPENDENT

By age 20, I lived a good life with a beautiful girlfriend. I wore nice clothes and rented a stylish home in Walnut Creek, an upper-middle-class area. I furnished the home with high end household items. I left no expense spared. I purchased all Maytag appliances. The stove was huge. I prepared lavish meals for breakfast and dinner. In the freezer, I could store almost 20 pounds of meat. My living room set was the talk of all my friends. When I threw get-togethers, everyone had plenty of room to sit on the plush sofas. For my lady friend and I, my king size bed offered us a spacious oasis. Finally, I owned two vehicles. My Monte Carlo was my pride and joy. I also had a new Honda 750 Supersport bike. Riding motorcycles was my hobby. I would put on my boots and jacket, gloves and helmet and go. I loved the feeling of the raw power of the bike between my legs.

I learned from the start to put everything I could in my name, my lease, phone, etc. By doing so, I would establish credit. From working at the bank I learned how having a credit record was an upcoming mean to financial success.

The braces were finally removed as my teeth were now straight.

Looking at myself in the mirror without a mouth full of metal made me smile. I clipped off the long curly hair and wore my hair short, combing it back. The last time I had my hair cut short was a punishment after I got caught with pot by the police. I didn't like short hair back then, maybe because my hair was cut despite how I felt. I also upgraded from glasses to contact lenses. Contacts were new and innovative. The first couple of times inserting the contacts required perseverance. My natural impulse was to close my eye as my finger approached. I had to force my eyes open until I got the hang of it.

Now looking at myself, short hair, contacts, and a metal-free mouth, I felt like a new man. With my new look came new confidence. I was back being the natural born leader. I asserted myself in conversations, when before I played the silent role. I had more influence over my friends. I was growing into adulthood.

WORK LIFE

I was working a warehouse job. My co-worker and I got along well. We were making scraps compared to what I knew the job was worth. We talked a few times about our wages, or I should say we vented about our wages. Everything was above ground until he told me a scheme. The scheme involved us manipulating the invoice manifest. It wasn't rocket science, all I needed to do was get a blank invoice slip and rewrite the quantities for parts ordered. I tried rewriting an invoice but got caught the first time. I didn't count on each invoice slip being numbered. I guess this was for tracking and billing purposes. When I turned in my slip to the office, it was logged with one number that fell out of sequence with the previous number and the following number. I don't know entirely, but they did find the discrepancy. The supervisor immediately called me in for a meeting. I was asked to explain the difference. Of course, I couldn't. I was terminated based on my actions.

I liked working with my hands. I couldn't see myself sitting in a cubicle all day. I loved the outdoors and the sun too much. I started a landscaping job. My Dad told me that it was seasonal work and I should look for another job. I did.

The second warehouse job I had was for a large linoleum company. Most of it was menial work. I unloaded trucks and had light inventory duties. I got raises on a regular basis. These types of jobs left little room for advancement and the money, regardless of raises, was peanuts.

The money wasn't enough so my criminal mindset in. I got fired for stealing. Again, I was hoping to live more comfortably and get some extra money. Due to thoughts of having bigger and better things, I would take unnecessary risks. All in all, I was okay financially and really didn't need to take such risks, yet criminal acts merely seemed easier and faster.

I look at myself as being a hustler. What I mean is that I will create a revenue source. I have always put my all into every job I ever worked. I made impressions on most of my employers. Good standing helped me to quickly move up in the rat race. With some jobs, I had opportunities to become a salesman but as with the linoleum job, trying to do something underhanded ruined excellent opportunities.

Home life wasn't a factor in my criminality. As I said I'm the only family member that has come to prison. My ambitiousness and desiring of nice things led to my criminal activities. I think in a way I disappointed my family.

JOYRIDING

One day while out with a friend, I took a 450 SL Mercedes Benz that was parked next to my 1978 Monte Carlo. I had wanted a Mercedes since I was knee-high to a grasshopper. My friend and I just had a great breakfast at Copper Skillet, in Dublin, California. I loved their hash browns and country fried steak. The car door to the Mercedes was unlocked. I opened the door and flipped down the visor looking for the keys. No luck. Something told me to check under the front seat. Sure enough, the keys were there. I immediately told my buddy to follow me, throwing him the keys to my Monte Carlo. He followed me and parked my car in another parking lot. We headed out to San Francisco.

I loved to go to San Francisco because it was a beautiful city, a city filled with trendsetters and diversity. My favorite spot to go was Fisherman's Wharf. People from all over the world visited Fisherman's Wharf. You could sample every kind of cuisine imaginable. The drive takes 45 minutes. I obeyed all speeding laws on the way. The last thing we wanted to do was bring attention to ourselves. We picked up three girls. It was a little weird because they were dressed like mimes. We hung out for a while walking up and down Fisherman Wharf. The weather changed and it started to get cold and windy. Such weather is common near the San Francisco Bay. It was time to go home. The girls seemed to have a good time hanging out with us. I asked the girls if they would give us a ride back. I flatly told them that car they had been riding in was stolen and we planned to leave it in San Francisco. They didn't believe me at first, but once they saw us wiping the car down for fingerprints, they knew we were honest. They agreed once we promised dinner. Turns out they were country girls from the outskirts of the Bay Area. It was a fun time.

SMALL BUSINESS OWNER

I was always good at working with wood. In school, I was an assistant to the woodshop instructor. One of my friends knew of a construction job working for an associate of his. I worked with this associate building a redwood deck. The house where we installed the deck was lavish. I burned to have enough money to buy a home, especially a similar high-end home.

We only had one job. When finished, this new work partner and I had no other jobs lined up. We sat around for a week doing nothing. I thought we could get more work with the right advertisement. I said, "I know how to get work. But we will be partners now." We called ourselves B&B construction, given that another company had a similar name so we thought the name similarity would help us. Neither of us had a business or contractor's license. Nonetheless, we went and printed business cards and flyers. I placed the flyers in mailboxes. Basically, I put flyers anywhere I felt customers may be found. I had to get our name out on the street. A most vital part of any business is advertising.

About three days after our advertising blitz the phone started ringing and jobs began to roll in. Soon, I didn't have time to handle the phones and be out on the job at the same time. I had to hire an answering service to handle all the calls our business was getting.

I separated from most of the people I knew in high school. For a time, I associated with one buddy from my younger years. In school, we had a very close bond. However, I needed to end that friendship. He and his girlfriend were selling cocaine. I wanted no part of that scene and the people it brought. I was working on making B&B a success. I developed friendships with more law-abiding business minded people. These new friends had their lives in order and seemed to be going in the right direction. We were all successful and equal. No one was a leader so to speak, but all had value to offer the others.

✖ ✖ ✖

Poverty shaped me. Growing up I was not ashamed of living off food stamps or the government housing that was provided to my mother and us. Still, I never wanted to be on government assistance or receive food stamps for myself. I have always strived to be a successful man. My need to accumulate money stemmed from my impoverished upbringing. I have a need for bigger and better things. This need would consume me and take over my thought patterns. I created various endeavors to build income. Acquiring money became my preoccupation. I put gathering it before further schooling or college. I sought another paycheck or additional cash from marijuana sales. Selling marijuana was the one gig I always kept.

SPA INSTALLATION JOB

You know the old saying that time flies when you're having fun. Well, that's true when running a successful business. I was in my second year of business. The jobs kept rolling in and I felt accomplished in life. My work schedule was rigorous, often 16 hours a day and always seven days a week. Such hours were required to complete the numerous contracts we secured. I had thoughts of hiring additional employees to help cover the workload, but finances wouldn't allow the expense. With company overhead, we remained in the red. Most profits were spent on tools, equipment, vehicle upkeep, etc. Nevertheless, running a company felt great.

Everything changed after I signed on for a spa installation job. The client commended us on the craftsmanship and detail we put into the job. He also admired our work ethic and character. In particular, he felt I was an upright person and he offered to buy into the business. He said that he knew many people with wealth and he could convince them to hire us. He would use his gorgeous spa as an example of our work. The man's wealth was evident to us and the terms favorable, so we agreed. I couldn't see much wrong with the deal.

He called a short while later informing me that he acquired a spa installation job in Danville, my old hometown. He set up a meeting with the client at the client's business in Dublin, a neighboring city. We met up without incident and signed all the necessary agreements. One clause of the contracts requires clients to pay for half of the job upfront. The clause was our insurance against buyer's remorse. I had to safeguard my purchase of materials. We learned of the need for this "insurance" the hard way, through struggles to get money from clients. As we met in this new client's Dublin office, the conversation and interaction were going fine. The client was reading through the contract. He stopped while reading over the paperwork and stated, "You know I don't have to pay you at the completion of the job?" I thought the statement odd and was taken aback. In reading through the agreement, he realized that our business operated without proper licensing. I wanted the job and I wanted to move forward with the signing. I replied, "Yes sir that is correct. I have you sign this form and I perform my job to high standards. After the job's completion, the next thing for you to do is pay me for the services." He then offered to use his own contractor's license number. Using his license felt like a safe bet so I agreed. The client asked one of his employees to bring the contractor license to us. After a few minutes, the employee came back without the license as he couldn't find it. The new client looked disgruntled. He then stated that if I could come up with two thousand dollars, he would help me get a license from Sacramento. I declined that deal in an instant. I didn't have that sort of money to get a license that had doubtful benefit to me. He told me when I did have the money to phone him and he would walk me through the licensing procedure. We started his job the next day.

The entire time I worked on installing the client's new spa, what he said about not having to pay me resonated through my head. I feared he would not pay us. I distrusted and disliked the man. I felt there was something tricky about him. I deliberated on the reasons why they couldn't come up with his contractor license number. The license should have been on multiple forms and letterheads. The man had me worried I was digging my own grave.

After completion of the job, he paid me with a check. I preferred cash and before each job requested cash from all clients. I submitted the check for deposit. It did not clear. When I called the bank to inquire what was the holdup, the bank notified me that the checking account the check was written from was opened up with funds from a personal check and that personal check had a 30-day hold on it. I had to wait the same amount of time for the check to clear. It felt like a slap in the face. These types of unnecessary complications are why I always requested cash. I felt like the client was purposely delaying my payment, deliberately screwing with me.

BLACK JACK LUCK

The check finally cleared. I breathed a sigh of relief. I felt like I beat the guy. I received the $1100. Luck was on my side. My construction partner and I decided to take a trip to Lake Tahoe to gamble.

On the drive up, all I could think about was how much money I was going to win. The way my luck was going, blackjack was my ticket to fast riches. I had been playing blackjack in casinos since I turned 18 years old. Even though we had the $1100, things were tight financially. I, personally, needed some extra money until we finished a Gazebo job we had.

Black Jack, a.k.a. 21, was the easiest game to play and win. I hit the tables and sat on the third chair looking toward the other players sitting near me. I wanted to gauge what type of players I faced. Not too long into gambling, my partner lost all the money he had, $550. I couldn't believe it. Now I felt like I had to win for both of us.

It was around 2 p.m. on a Saturday afternoon. I sat at that table for hours. The momentum shifted back and forth from the dealer to us gambling at the table. I would hit some good runs and stack a few hundred; however, I couldn't reach my goal of $1400.

By 9 a.m. Sunday morning, I was out of money. The house is bound to win I suppose after that amount of time at a table. I walked off with my head toward the ground. The walk of shame. I know many have taken it before me. I had no money whatsoever. I nothing left for gas or for a meal. I looked through the car hoping I had stashed some money somewhere. To my luck, I had my business checks safe in the dash compartment. Even though checks weren't accepted at most of the places, we were able to find a meal. At the self-service gas station, I filled up and handed the cashier a check. The clerk refused at first but I had no cash so he had to accept the alternative of taking the check. We then hit the road and headed home.

The next day I went to work thinking of the predicament I was now in. I didn't have enough money to complete the contracts at hand. These new financial straits were the last thing I needed. I begin to put my focus on the spa client who issued me a time-delayed check. I felt anger at his way of addressing me regarding my not having a license. I thought him arrogant and that he put unnecessary burdens on others. He never paid any interest for the wait time on his check to clear. Thinking about this client made me more irate by the minute. Slowly the thought of every-thing that had gone wrong in my life pointed towards him, his arrogance and his wealth. I decided to rob the client. Of course, I understand now I was irrational in my attributions of guilt.

The client had two five-gallon water jugs full of money sitting next to his fireplace. They were full of bills and coins. He noticed me staring at them while at his home so he explained the intent of the jugs. The client and the client's son were jointly saving money to buy the son his first car, once the son turned 16. As an adult, I had never robbed anyone. As a kid, as mentioned, I broke into a few homes but I hadn't tried such a thing as an adult. I didn't care about of the good intention to be had with the jugs of money. In fact, frustrating that purpose may have egged on my own desire to have the coins for myself. I decided to rob this client's house of those coins.

MY CRIME - FEBRUARY 13, 1980

I went over the plan with my co-worker. It would be a quick in and out job. All we wanted to do was grab the jugs and split. He thought it was a good idea also. We decided guns would be needed in case there was any trouble. I have never shot anyone, nor planned on doing so. The only time I had shot a gun was skeet shooting with neighbors while younger. I had a buddy that had a few firearms so I called him to borrow a couple. Luckily, he didn't ask too many questions. He loaned me a .22 caliber rifle and a .38 caliber Smith & Wesson pistol. The guns had no ammo so I went to Gemco to buy bullets. Later, I also purchased nylon stockings and beanie hats, gloves and rope. I wanted to be prepared for every contingency. Little did I know the surprises ahead.

I was restless the night before with thoughts about our plan. I finally dozed off to sleep. Tuesday arrived. It was February 13, 1980. It was the day of the heist. I woke up before the break of dawn. There was a gazebo installation job to complete and I was scheduled to meet with potential clients later in the day.

Both of the day's tasks went well. I installed a lattice on the gazebo and I secured a new job to build a deck. The new clients even paid me half the money on the spot. Walking out of their home, I knew I was now free to walk into the former client's home and proceed to rob it. I hoped to knock on the door, just like I did as a kid, and after finding no one home, simply enter the house and walk out with the 5-gallon jugs filled with coins and cash. Yet Murphy's Law, that whatever can go wrong will, manifested itself in full force that Tuesday evening.

I had no other vehicle, so we decided to use the company truck. Driving the truck left us at a disadvantage. Even though we didn't have any branding on the truck, the guy knew the vehicle. We parked the truck on a dirt road next to the Danville fire department. The road was about a block and a half away from the guy's house.

I sat in the truck for a few minutes sweating. My first thoughts were to call it off, but I kept getting pissed by what the client put us through. We decided it was time. We were all set with our nylon stocking face masks. We wore the beanies to cover our heads. We also wore turtleneck sweaters. All that could be seen of us was our eyes. Everything we wore was expendable. We had intentions to burn all the clothing afterward. Neither of us had a record, but we wore gloves just in case.

There was not a lot of traffic in the area. We didn't think it necessary to hide the firearms, so we walked with the guns in hand. I had the rifle and my partner had the .38 special and rope. He also carried a buck knife in his belt to cut the rope. Our plan was to be prepared for anything. It took us only a few minutes to reach the house.

The first thing I did was cut the phone line. There would be no calling for help on my watch. As we started toward the house, a station wagon pulled into the driveway. A man and woman were in the car. I had never seen the pair before. My partner and I looked at each other. Although we didn't speak, we seemed to agree that things were going wrong from the start. We paused for a moment looking at each other. I motioned for us to leave. He seemed to think about it and finally shook his head no. How different my life would have been if we did leave.

Now, we knew there were definitely people at the house, people we didn't count on being there. Further, we understood, if guests were arriving there also would be hosts. While these thoughts flooded my mind, we met a greater surprise, four people appeared from the side of the house and faced us. My partner reacted quickly. In a threatening voice, he yelled for them to not move and get back into the house. I then popped up. I shouted in a disguised voice for them to get back into the house. They all complied immediately.

We entered the house with the four in front of us. There were two men and two women. My partner made the two men lay on the carpet in the family room. He tied their hands behind their backs. The ladies were told to sit at the dinner table and not move. My heart was pounding a million beats a second. Out of the corner of my eye, I noticed a kid in the house. He was told to not move and stay seated on the couch. I stood there with my rifle drawn and made sure no one moved. One of the ladies sitting at the table looked at me. She kept peering at me even though all she could see was my eyes. She looked at me intently as if she knew me. She then asked, "How did you get yourself into a predicament like this." I sort of felt she was sincere, but there I stood, nonetheless, looking like a terrorist. I replied in a confident filled voice of intimidation, "Easy!"

My partner searched out the house. Within seconds he returned shaken and startled. "The house is surrounded," he yelled.

"There are cops everywhere. They got floodlights on every window!" "How the hell could there be cops here?" I replied. We weren't in the house for more than a couple of minutes. That news was a shock to me.

I quickly ran to a window and looked outside. I pulled the curtain back slowly. I was blinded by the floodlights. I promptly shut the curtain and tried to regain my vision. I then ran back to the dining room. My partner stood there motionless. His lips quivered as he asked, "What are we going to do?" Neither of us had planned for any of this occurring. I was no robber and these types of plots were never explained in TV shows yet there was nothing else to do except plan our exit. I said, "We're getting out of here." I pulled up one of the men from the floor and motioned for my partner to grab someone. I thought we would get away if we could make it back to the truck. Two persons volunteered to go with us. The police were notorious for shooting people back then so the plan was to use the people as human shields. I told my partner to stay in the house and I was going to pull the parked car in the driveway closer so my partner could exit with the additional hostage. He agreed. I had no idea who the man was I held tight to me but I knew the police weren't playing around. We exited the house. My gun was in hand. I didn't want to hurt him but I had no intention of allowing the police to shoot me. Plus, my mind was set on not giving myself up. I had no intention of going to jail and I thought I would get away.

Everything seemed to move in slow motion as I walked outside with the man as hostage. Everywhere I looked were police. Their floodlights shined directly in my face and covered every inch of the house. My partner was still in the house. I hoped he wouldn't do anything stupid. From the driver's side, I pushed the guy into the station wagon and over and into the passenger seat. I got into the driver's seat. The car was in the driveway but

I wanted it closer so my partner could jump in. I started the car and inched up the driveway to a spot beneath the awning. My partner saw me and quickly exited the house with a female hostage in tow. He jumped into the back seat with her and I began backing the car out of the driveway. Suddenly, it was as if a fourth of July celebration began. Explosions started going off. Bullets rained in on us. Glass from the exploding car windows was flying into our faces and all around us. The sounds were deafening as percussion grenades exploded. Why were they shooting at us? I yelled, "Everyone get down!" As I said that, I felt a sharp pain in my arm. I lowered my head as much as I could while still controlling the vehicle. I could tell they were shooting at me and I was surprised. I only had intentions of getting away. I continued to see explosions and gun barrels burst in front of me as we drove down the street. We reached a cul-de-sac so I swerved the car into a chained gate hoping that I could gain exit that way. The station wagon easily proceeded through the chained gate. The car bumped around through the grassy field of a school. I bounced around in the car trying to maintain control of it while looking for way to exit the school field. The guy that sat next to me yelled, "Did you get hit?" He seemed to repeat this question over and over as I didn't respond to him. I had to stay focused on the terrain in front of me. I could tell he was sincere with his concern. The car seemed to swerve left and right. They had shot out the tires on the car so it was extremely difficult maintaining control. I didn't know the area or school I was driving through. I kept asking the guy next to me, "Can I get out this way?" He responded, "I don't think so." I drove as far around one of the building as I could searching for an exit but there was none to be found. The tires were shot out on the car. The rim started to dig into the grass now. We were going nowhere fast. The car slowed to a crawl. I still had not given up hope of an escape. I put the car in park and jumped out. I left the rifle on the front seat. I hopped over a fence and ran towards a vacant lot. I heard shots being fired at me. Bullets seemed to whiz just inches above my head. Some of the bullets were so close I could feel the wind as they passed. What I didn't know was the entire time my partner had been shooting at the officers. I yelled at him, "Get down now!" as I realized we were in the crossfire between two groups of police. When my partner stopped shooting, everything became eerily silent. I wondered if I was dead. The ache in my arm told me I was alive. My heart was pounding and I was soaked with sweat and blood. Realizing I was shot increased my panic. The surrounding area was covered with the sight of flashlight beams. I saw I had gone the right way and the company truck was within sight.

My partner crawled on his belly toward me and we crawled in the direction of a stack of tractor tires piled on top of each other. We climbed inside. The police had brought in dogs. I hoped that they thought we had fled and they would continue on looking for us elsewhere. It seemed like an eternity that we sat there waiting for them to leave. However, the cops didn't leave, they only got closer. I heard the dog handler say, "Come on boy, find 'em." I never saw the dog but eventually, lights flowed into the tires like they were transparent. I heard the officer say, "Get out slowly with your hands up." Raising our hands, we both climbed out of the tires. We were slammed to the ground and handcuffed.

I was placed in the back of a squad car. I had a gunshot wound to my left arm. While sitting in the car, another officer covered in mud ordered the driver to shine his light down on me. The second officer pointed his hand at me as if his hand was a pistol. He then pulled an invisible trigger while making a shooting noise. He shouted, "You bastards tried to kill me!" His pant leg seemed to have a bullet hole in it. The assumption being that the hole happened when my partner was shooting in their direction. They cut off the light and slammed the door.

I was transported to the hospital and treated for my wounds. The nurse described the gunshot wound as "through and through." It only needed to be cleaned and sutured. I was handcuffed to the bed. A group of police officers stood by as the medical staff attended to my injuries. A cast was put on my left arm. The cast ran from my armpit down to my wrist. I was chained to the hospital bed at both ankles.

My dad was granted permission by a judge to see me while I was in the hospital. That was the worse feeling of my life. I was discharged from the hospital after four days.

✗ ✗ ✗

I feel my arrest was a blessing and a curse. A blessing because I'm still alive. A curse because of where I have been for the past 38 years. What prompted the police to come as quickly as they did was a combination of my having cut the phone line to the house and the homeowners having had set up security systems due to previous burglaries. I guess God has funny ways of preventing us from doing further damage in life.

12

___

FREE ON BAIL

I was processed and booked into the station jail. I was assigned a court-appointed attorney for representation. He came to the sub-station to visit with me. The attorney was skeptical of my chances against the charges. He listed them off:

Count 1: Kidnap for the purpose of robbery

Count 2: Attempted murder on a peace officer

Count 3: Robbery with use of a gun

The charge of attempted murder had no grounds. The attempted murder was based on the officer who had a small caliber bullet hole in the leg of his trousers. The assertion was either my partner or I shot him. I believe with the number of shots the officers took, the bullet was from one of their guns.

My bail was set at $87,000. I had no way of paying that kind of money up front, even if I took out loans and borrowed from everyone I knew. Two days later I went for arraignment at municipal court. The judge noted that it was my first offense and I wasn't a flight risk. He reduced my bail to $20,000, which was still a huge sum of money but I thought I could gather it. I felt it would be easier for me to fight the charges from the streets rather than from prison. I began making calls.

There weren't many people in my life I could go to for money. I had one close friend from high school who did have some money and I made a deal with him to work in exchange for bail help. This kindhearted person agreed to loan me a majority of the $20,000. The rest of the funds were gathered from everyone I knew.

I made bail. I was glad to be free. I worked on weekends at my friends' ranch. It was light and simple work, but I did these menial tasks with a smile on my face.

I continued to work as a carpenter and did various handyman tasks to keep an income coming in. The court dates seemed to be scheduled every three months which gave me plenty of time to live. It was a back and forth battle between the multiple motions my lawyer and the D.A. seemed to file against each other. I honestly had no defense. From what the D.A. said it was the easiest slam dunk case he ever had. We basically were caught red-handed with hostages in tow. The hope was to resolve the charges via a plea-bargain.

13

MARRIAGE PROPOSAL

I had a lot of crushes on TV stars growing up. I loved Jaclyn Smith; her role on Charlie's Angel's brought many smiles to my nights. There was also Brook Shields. Her overall persona attracted me. In the real world, I can only think of four women that captivated me. With each one of them, I felt I had true love. I asked each of them for their hand in marriage.

While out on bail and I met a new woman. She was only 18 while I was 22. We had a lot in common. I was living at the house of the friend that bailed me out. She would come over often to visit. She was a wonderful lady. At the time, she was enrolled at U.C. Berkeley. Together we enjoyed athletics, such as working out and water skiing. We played tennis and often would play with her parents at a local racquet club.

After a few months of dating, she moved in with me. Yet the ultimate nightmare arrived. I had to go back to jail. She didn't miss a visit. It was a breath of fresh air seeing her, despite the situation. She gave me hope for the future and my new life. I felt with every ounce of me that this was my soul mate.

I ended up taking a plea bargain for 7 to life. It was a "decent deal," said my lawyer. My girlfriend was in court and waved at me. It gave me reassurance that I did not have to face everything alone. I was eager to get the court process over. The plea was conditioned on the district attorney dropping the attempted murder and attempted assault on a peace officer charges. I felt those two charges were the most serious and my lawyer agreed. I took that plea bargain in October 1980. My lawyer sold it to me with the hope of me getting out after seven years. Here we are 38 years later and I still fight for my freedom.

When I was a young man, I committed the only felony of my life, which resulted in a 7-to-life sentence for the crime of kidnap robbery. I feel up until that point I was a law-abiding citizen. I was in pursuit of the American dream. I have always felt I am a genuine and an authentic man. I am an honest, compassionate, loving, and very trustworthy person. My friends, family, and associates have always been able to count on me for anything. I have been there mentally and financially to support all those involved in my life. My prayers are for another chance at life. I feel I have wasted many years in prison that I could have used to make a positive difference in the world. Here I sit 38 years later as a result of one bad decision.

I sat waiting in the county jail for about a month before being transferred. I arrived at San Quentin reception. My girlfriend filled out the visiting form and was approved. On the first visit from my girlfriend, I proposed to her and she accepted my hand in marriage. We were to have a jailhouse wedding.

Part of the marriage protocol required her to write a letter on why she wanted to marry me and to state the reason for my incarceration. A lot of convicts lie about their sentence and the time remaining on their sentence so the corrections department requires would be mates to write a detailed understanding of their loved one's offenses. The letter was supposed to be sent to my prison counselor, but it mistakenly came to me. I read the beautiful letter she had written. I felt a sincere and genuine expression of love clearly communicated in her words. I was at a loss and felt unworthy of such a wonderful person. I loved this woman with every ounce of me.

I began to think that it would be unfair of me to ask her to put life on hold for an uncertain duration of time while I languished in prison. I was contemplating one of the hardest decisions I would have to make in my life. In the end, because of the uncertainty of my sentence, I decided not to marry her. She objected and we fought over my decision. Our correspondence dwindled over the next years. Eventually, she was out of my life.

MEETING MY WIFE

I had a friend that worked at Longs Drugs. I asked her if she would create a flyer for me as I was seeking a pen-pal. I sent her a photo I had taken on the lower yard at San Quentin State Prison. I hoped I would get many responses. Before she could put the flyer up her co-worker saw the photo. Her co-worker was adamant that the flyer didn't go up. She would become my pen-pal.

In her first letter to me, she relayed how she had told our mutual friend, "You're not putting this up in the lunch room. I'm going to write him!" Things progressed in our letter writing, so we set up a visiting date. I had a buddy that worked in the visiting room. He had a table reserved for us. He placed a vase with two roses that I had cut earlier from the San Quentin Garden Chapel, a religious meeting chapel at the prison. Our first visit was on December 24th, 1983. Our visit went as well as possible. She began to come to the prison every weekend. We talked to each other about why I was in prison and the potentiality of how long I could be here. She fully understood my situation and had no objections.

MARRIED LIFE

I felt in my heart that I was ready and had found the one. I proposed to her with no reserve. She accepted my hand in marriage and the wedding date was set. I then contacted the Family Visiting coordinator and informed her of my upcoming wedding. I hoped to secure a family visit date that coincided with our wedding. I wanted the consummation of the marriage to play out similar to a free person's wedding.

Our wedding occurred in the non-contact visiting area. The same area is now used for the reception of new inmates at San Quentin. KRON News, a local TV station in the Bay Area, wanted to do a segment on jailhouse weddings. They contacted the San Quentin's Public Information Officer and asked if they could film a wedding. They were granted permission to do so. Our wedding just happened to coincide with the time of the filming. We were asked if we would allow KRON to film our marriage. We agreed and signed the waivers. It was actually a good idea because our kids and grandkids could watch it for years to come. The news crew went to my fiancé's home and asked her questions about our relationship. The news crew was also allowed in prison. They shot b-roll of me working at the print shop. They filmed me going in and out of my West Block housing unit and cell. Crazy enough, they were granted permission to take footage from the gun rail above. From, the gun rail they took a long distance shot of my soon-to-be bride driving her van up to the family visiting cottage. The final shot was of my now wife and I, entering the family visiting cottage together.

We married in June of 1984. By the end of 1985, we were contemplating bringing a child into the world. Because we were both raised in broken homes, we had a dilemma. We did not want the same for our future children. She and I had plenty of talks about staying together no matter what. I thought it best to wait until I was out of prison for children. I wanted to be there every step of the way. Unfortunately, prison wouldn't allow it.

After we were together for about a year and a half, we found out that my wife was pregnant. I am a firm believer that everyone should go through parenting school before bringing a child into the world. A tremendous amount of dedication and finances are required to raise a child.

Our first son was born on December 10, 1986. He was beautiful. Now, the pressure of parenting by proxy was at hand. The weekly visiting schedule helped and the family visits, which happened once every three months, helped out a lot. Family visits allowed me three days of family time and bonding. I tried to make it a vacation for my wife. I did all the chores and I cooked all the meals. Cooking has always been a passion of mine. I also changed the diapers every chance I could. I welcomed the challenge, the opportunity to be helpful.

Our second son, an equally handsome boy, was born on June 28, 1990. Family visits were a lifesaver and weekend visits allowed for continued bonding and also socializing with others.

Families would stop by and congratulate us. They would comment on how handsome our sons were. On one occasion while changing my son in the visiting room, he let out a burst of urine. The saying is true, "When you got to go, you got to go." It was one of the funniest moments I can remember. So, I learned to ask him when I heard his stomach rumble, "Did you poo, or was that gas?" With the most innocent of looks, he would reply, "gas."

Our family visits were far and few between but I looked at it as a time to bond with my sons. Family visits would allow my wife to see me interact with my sons. Some of my heartfelt moments were when my sons helped me cook in the kitchen. They would handle the small details, like toss scraps or retrieving items from the fridge, with an adorable zeal. I remember my oldest said to me, "Dad I like your cooking."

My youngest was around a year old, the day of our last family visit. On that day, my boys and I awoke before mom and played. I fed my son a bottle. My wife awoke around 10 a.m. I cooked my wife her favorite breakfast, the same breakfast I would cook for her each visit, Eggs Benedict.

By 10 p.m., while feeding my youngest a bottle and listening to my wife, I passed out. I was either nudged by my wife or just re-awaken. She asked me if I was going to listen to her. I was exhausted. I realized I was tired after a day with the children on a mere family visit. I considered the magnitude of what my wife must go through daily.

16

SAN FRANCISCO CABLE CARS

I did the best I could to send money to the family. I was fortunate to end up in a prison that had a hobby shop. The hobby shop is a place where you can order materials to do wood-work. I started making miniature cable cars, modeled from the cable cars in San Francisco. I also made miniature pianos and jewelry boxes. I created three different size cable cars which sold primarily at the hobby store at San Quentin State prison. With the business mind I have always possessed, I hired three inmates that had no outside financial support and no wood-working experience. They were good, diligent men that simply made a mistake and wound up in prison. Each man assembled and glued the cable cars. As a result, I was able to send a minimum of $200 a month home to my wife. During the holiday season, I would gross $1000 a month. My miniature cable cars enabled me to help my wife purchase Christmas presents for the kids. Even though I was incarcerated, as a man and husband I still felt I had a duty to provide for my family. I feel I was the best lover, father, and friend possible despite my prison incarceration handicap. In fact, through our dual efforts, in 1986, we were able to save enough money to buy a home. Despite being in prison, I was transforming my life into that of a successful man.

17

DIVORCE

By 1991, I could tell that my wife was tired of the routine. Something just didn't seem the same during our visits. She sat right in front of me, but I still felt distant from her. I loved her with all my heart, so I was at a loss. Prison can wear the best of us down. It wasn't designed to hold families together but tear them apart. Neither of us was to blame, but divorce was on the horizon. I thought a good way to show my wife that I loved her was to allow her to live her life. I wanted her to be free from the prison confines of my life. That way my kids could have a father there with them every night instead of just weekends. It was indeed the hardest decision I had to make in my life. It would, in fact, deny my part in the lives of my boys. My oldest son was about four at the time. My youngest was just rounding a year old.

I explained the situation to my immediate family. Some didn't understand, but divorce was what I felt was right. I reached out to my Dad and my friends to ask each to help support my children. I asked them to bring my children to visit with me from time to time. This was done so my wife wouldn't have to see the pain on my face that divorce was causing me. The divorce finalized that same year.

My friends and Dad helped for a short period of time with visits, but that ended in 1993. No one had the time to bring my kids up to see me. It was a devastating period in my life. I wrote the boys on a regular basis but could only hope that they got my letters. Up to this day, I have never stopped writing to them nor sending gifts.

18

LOSS OF HOPE

D rug use was not prominent in my life, especially at the time of my crime. Yes, I used, but my usage was more so a holiday from life's routine. On the streets, I was not addicted to any drug. I sold marijuana and, at times, other drugs, but I never allowed drugs to grab hold of me. In prison, it was the same. I was more into bodybuilding and working out. Exercise was my greatest stress reliever. I worked out six days a week until in 1998, the year California Department of Corrections decided to remove the weights. At the time, then-Governor Wilson during a tour of prisons saw the shape inmates were in. After the tour, he made a press statement to the notion that prison bred caged animals. His guards stood no chance of defending themselves against such beasts. The positive effects for inmates of weightlifting were twisted and sullied out of fear. He signed an order to remove weights from prison.

At first, the state placed a limit on how much weight we could use. To be able to work out, the state also required the viewing of weight training instructional videos. Finally, correctional officials systematically removed all weights from prisons. Having a stress reliever in weightlifting was sufficient, so drug use wasn't on my mind. Also, I had a day job assigned to me by the prison. I didn't want to miss any time or money, so I hunkered down and pursued my business as a stress reliever.

I had my life in order. I went to my scheduled progress hearing. The Parole Board found me suitable to be released into society. Everyone was excited, including me. During this period, the governor can revoke your parole grant for basically whatever reason he deems. This was a terrifying period for me due to no lifer, at that time, ever clearing the governor's signature. We were called "political prisoners." As it happened, the governor denied my parole.

I lost hope as a result. I felt powerless. I honestly thought that I would never see society or home. I began using drugs for comfort and, eventually, spiraled into misery and started heavy drug use. I called my family and friends and told them I was never coming home. I told both not to write to me anymore, and, by then, I was no longer contacting them. I slowly became a drug addict.

19

DRUGS AND TVS

During this period life was overwhelming. Crack and meth use was a daily thing for me. To make matters worse, I was just getting out of Administrative Segregation, the hole, after four months. I had been charged with "Conspiracy to Commit Bodily Injury to a Correctional Officer." That was a serious offense. Apparently, a black prison gang called 415 had plans to commit the act. I honestly had nothing to do with the conspiracy. Nor did I have a residue of knowledge about the plot yet I had to endure the entire disciplinary process. Prison staff was to investigate the likelihood of my participation. Please know that in prison, you're guilty until proven innocent.

Meanwhile, I was in a cell 23 hours a day. Eventually, the pain ended. I was cleared of the rules violation and, without an apology, released back to the mainline.

Now everything I had accomplished was gone. By being in the hole, I lost my prison job and my hobby shop woodwork enterprise. I needed a new income source. Prison offers opportunities for revenue, either legal or illegal. I chose the legal realm. I knew a guy that had a few TVs stocked up. I propositioned him to buy the TVs at a discounted price. I slowly began to buy 13-inch color TVs and rent them out to other inmates. All the enterprise required was for me to keep an inventory of how many TVs were rented out, to whom the TVs were rented out, and the balance owed to me by each renter. I had a monthly rental fee of two cans of Bugler tobacco. Cans of tobacco sold for $5 at this time. At my peak, I owned and rented out 22 13-inch TVs. I acquired that many TVs in one year.

The TV repairman had 16-inch color TVs that he wanted me to rent out for him. He didn't like dealing with inmates because of the games they played. I agreed to do so. I also needed his help to maintain my own TVs. Thus, with the additional 16-inch TVs, I was renting approximately 38 TVs on a monthly basis.

The income was great. I was profiting on average 60 cans of Bugler at $5 a can so basically a $300 monthly cycle. I still needed to expand. I created a T.V. guide business and had 145 customers. They each paid a pouch of Bugler a month, which cost $1.45. The T.V. guide business brought in revenue of $210 a month. From both endeavors, I was making $510 a month.

The TV enterprise was how I supported myself and my ever-growing crack and meth habit. I understood I should have been sending the money home, but drugs had me. I couldn't wait to get back to my cell to get high. There were small clusters of inmates lined up outside my cell waiting on me. They knew my money was good. I would easily spend a couple hundred a week getting high.

DRUG TRANSPORT

Inmates are either bussed here or arrive in a van, as San Quentin is a Northern California reception center. San Quentin also serves to house general population inmates and holds the men on California's Death Row.

The inmates that were lined up outside my cell generally had some connection to the reception inmates. The reception inmates came directly from the county jails or other prisons. Drugs were clandestinely transported by reception inmates to San Quentin. New batches of prisoners came through Monday through Friday, yet drug contraband arriving with them was never guaranteed. There were days when nothing came in. We called those "dry days." Dry days happened mostly on weekends when no new arrivals pulled up.

Dealing with my addiction was rough during those dry periods. The quality of the crack and meth also varied. Some of the stuff was really good; other times you got crap. I had various connections to ensure that I got the best. Of course, I had inmates who had their old ladies bring drugs in through the visiting room also. I did everything under the sun to get high.

FUNCTIONING ADDICT FOR JESUS

I had no goals or cares at this time. My mental state was focused on my total destruction at any cost. If I died from a drug overdose, it would be an end to my misery. I used crack and meth on a daily basis which made my tolerance grow. I hoped I would use so much that my brain would explode. By overdosing, I would not have to suffer or endure the pain of prison anymore. I thought about my family every time I got high. The pain of separation and not seeing them made me delve deeper into usage. I was a full-blown addict and could care less if I died. I would have full week runs of getting high all day, every day. I would use until my body gave out and crashed.

At that time, I classified myself as a functioning addict. No matter how I felt, I still got up and went to work. The psychosis part about my addiction was, I would applaud myself as to how I could maintain responsibilities while high. I continued this drug-induced state until a couple months into 2002. The only thing that stopped me was being a drummer in the church. I felt I was disrespecting my Lord and Savior by coming to church loaded. I was representing the church while the drugs were coursing through my veins. There was a sermon one week in which I felt God was talking directly to me. The preacher said, "Whatever you might do outside of this church is your own business. But remember, outside you all represent the body of this church and not just yourself." I took that to heart and had to step down from the church with hopes of getting my life together.

Shortly after stepping down from the church I was approached by a correctional officer while at work. The C.O. told me I was being placed into Administrative Segregation for suspicion of giving an order to have an inmate jumped. Allegedly the inmate who was jumped was a snitch.

Here again, I found myself in the hole pending investigation. I stayed there until I was transferred to Old Folsom State Prison in 2002. It goes without saying, but while in Administrative Segregation I was drug-free. Additionally, the transfer to Old Folsom from San Quentin helped to maintain my sobriety. I was sober for almost a year.

During this time, my mother passed. I received a share of the family mineral rights. The value of my inheritance was around $7700. My plan was to pay off my debts. I chose to give my two sons $500 each. I owed my sister $1500, so I paid her off in full. I paid my best friend $500 for the filing of a writ, a legal petition. The writ was an appeal filed against the Board of Prison terms for denying my parole date. Sadly, I blew the rest of the money on drugs and quarterly packages. Drugs had called me and told me they were my friend.

Whenever I would go on a drug binge, it seemed I would I find myself in Administrative Segregation. I was placed in the hole again. This time for another conspiracy charge. I was there for seven months. The blessing was I was able to re-establish my relationship with my Lord and Savior Jesus Christ. I studied the scriptures daily. I would wake my day up with God's word and wisdom. I shared my Daily Bread, In Touch, and Discovery Bible Reading Guide with the other inmates there. It seems that most of us in the hole were lost and needed spiritual guidance.

Despite being locked in a cell for almost 24 hours each day. I found the peace that I was seeking. I had peace and joy in my life and heart for the first time in decades. This time when I was released back to the mainline I continued my relationship with God and not the drugs. I began seminary classes through Golden Gate Baptist Theological Seminary School. Our church had arranged all the paperwork to facilitate these classes. The church offered any inmate who desired to learn about our Lord an avenue to do so through college courses.

Study and prayer helped me tremendously. I worked on my fellowship with the Lord each and every day. I was growing stronger in my relationship with God. But I was still weak. I watched a friend do a shot of meth. I was weak in fighting my addiction and in not more than two hours I had a needle in my arm. The rush came back and all that I had gained seemed to be lost. I didn't leave my cell for three weeks. All I could muster up to do was go to chow and the shower. I was just chasing the high of meth. I was lucky I didn't lose my job as a result. I would call in sick every day instead of reporting in. I lied and told my supervisor I had the Norovirus. The Norovirus makes you have diarrhea and vomiting at the same time. It's highly contagious and had been going around the prison. My supervisor didn't think twice about me not coming in. I would do one big shot each night after the guards secured the lock bar and the tier was clear. I would do this for many nights straight until my body would shut down.

Today, I am an usher at the Protestant chapel at San Quentin. I love the church. Occasionally, I fill in on the drums for the "praise and worship" ceremony held for reception inmates.

I started going to different classes and programs offered at the prison. I enrolled in another college called Patten University. My goal was to earn a second A.A. degree; my first being a theology degree. I studied hard and earned A grades on my tests and papers. I love to read. I believe reading more has helped my grades and my mind.

I also am a drummer in a prison band. We play all sorts of music from rock and roll, rhythm and blues, and even classical. Our performances occur in the yard. Music is a way to help me get my life together.

22

LOVE AND HUMAN KINDNESS

Thoughts of staying drug-free for my family gave me strength. My ex-wife and I hadn't spoken in years. My relationship with the kids was estranged. My youngest didn't want anything to do with me. The boys ended up being raised by a step-dad. I tried everything possible to be involved in their lives. I send letters constantly as well as gifts when I can afford the expense. I know such items are not the same as fatherly love and parenting but I, at least, want the boys to know I always think of them.

In 2005, I was blessed with a letter from my boy's mother. She wanted to bring the kids to the prison for a visit. She wanted the boys in my life and I in theirs. It was the kindest thing anyone has done for me while I have been in prison. The boys and I had a wonderful visit. It was very emotional seeing them after all the years. I remember sweating profusely before the visit. It felt like I was seeing them for the first time. I received some flak and anger from my youngest boy. He was very upset that I was still in prison. He, of course, has a right to be. Children need their father at home. There was no excuse nor did I try to create an excuse for my absence. He told me, "If you put my brother and me first in your life, you would've been out by now!" I took that to heart and have done all I can since then to come home. I was blessed with a grandson by my oldest son in 2016. I am very proud of the job my ex-wife did raising our children. Both of them have excelled in life. They both have college degrees. They have blossomed into outstanding men. I am very proud of them. I thank God for shining his light on them. The good outcome of their lives has shown me that a rose can grow through concrete.

From the time of my divorce, I rejected all outside female contact. I didn't want to start a relationship with a woman. I was afraid of hurting another woman emotionally like I did my first wife. It wasn't until a few years ago that I agreed to correspond with someone. Through our writing, we have grown very close. We are now planning to get married. This marriage will last the duration of my days on earth. She is a beacon of hope for me. I hope to be released soon. I will spend the rest of my days thanking her for making me whole again.

23

LIFE LOOKING IN THE MIRROR

My life took a tragic turn from a terrible decision. It was one day and one moment in time. I have so much regret and empathy for the family I robbed. I have empathy for the officer almost injured in the events of that day. I keep them and their families in my prayers. If you take anything from my story, please realize that it only takes a split second to throw your life away.

I have learned to be proud of the man I see in the mirror. I do wonder what I could have been, but I prefer to look at the steps in life I have made. I'm a recovering addict. Without the trials and tribulations, I have endured I would be less of a man than I am today and am destined to be. I am a recovering addict who has by God's grace found acceptance of who I am and what I have been.

I am studying business for my release. I imagine myself getting a real estate license and flipping houses or perhaps obtaining a wholesale license to sell cars. I studied Spanish for the past few years as I see the demographics of the country change. I feel knowing a second language will only be a benefit. I possess a solid work ethic and I know how to prioritize my responsibilities first. My father instilled this work ethic in me. He never missed a day of work. Whether he was sick or just burnt out, he still rolled out of bed and did his job.

I hope this story will have a positive effect on you. I ask that you stop and think before making any rash choices. Our choices can have never predicted or conceived of ripple effects. These effects can reach into the lives of future generations, your own kin, community, and not to mention your own life. I pray you can live vicariously through my life without making the same mistake.

MOUTHPIECE: BOOK FOUR OF THE MY CRIME SERIES RETROSPECTIVE

PUBLISHER'S WRITE UP FOR MOUTHPIECE

Mouthpiece is a brutally told biographical sketch of an incarcerated pimp, in prison for human trafficking. Raw boasts and brazen inner-city tales litter the story's violent, unrepentant landscape.

Like a marked man, Mouthpiece keeps after the reader with a cold perspective. Money is the aim and young women are the product.

Bullets fly, tears drop, and children watch, Mouthpiece communicates the pride and prejudices of a warrior-pimp seizing plunder, camaraderie, and a demigod sense of self, through violence, street credentials, and psychological manipulation.

The East Oakland Times, LLC welcomes you to purchase the book today. "Mouthpiece" can be found on Amazon, Audible, and at www.crimebios.com

✖ ✖ ✖

Mouthpiece

I was around twenty-two when I got shot for the second time. I was out spending time with this female who was basically giving me money. I had worked some things out to where every month, the bank was giving me almost three bands (three thousand dollars.) It wasn't much, just a little chump change I used to buy guns and some syrup to sip.

I asked my mom to take me to a bank branch in Alameda, about twenty miles from Richmond. Now I could have gone to any branch of this particular bank and collected my money, but I am meticulous and only wanted to use the bank branch in Alameda.

Reluctantly, my mom agreed. However, the entire time we were in the car, she was ranting and raving about how I was out in the streets too much and needed to slow down. She was preaching about how I needed to stop doing the stuff I was doing and get my life together.

Needless to say, I had no desire to hear all of her complaining. It got so bad that I just asked her to drop me off at my cousin's house, which of course, she refused to do. In fact, she demanded that I listen to her.

Eventually, it became so overwhelming that I threatened to just jump out of the car at the next light if she did not stop her talk. Finally, she relented and took me to my cousin's. Before she left, I gave her a few dollars which she gladly took from me.

✖ ✖ ✖

At my cousin's, I immediately started smoking weed as soon as I entered the house. They were already blazing and getting high, yet that was nothing out of the ordinary. Eventually, I got around to asking my cousin to take me to the bank. He was reluctant but relented. His one demand was that I leave my gun at the house. Now leaving my gun was something that I just didn't do, and I normally would have had a fit just because he asked, but I gave in because he said that he would take his gun instead.

We did argue over who would do the driving. He had a two-door Benz and I was dying to get behind the wheel. Of course, with it being his car, he won that argument. So, to relax, I stretched out in the back seat with my head laying on the window. I am not sure how long I laid there because I was high. Now one truth about driving is that whoever is doing the driving is supposed to watch the rearview mirror. The driver is the eyes of the car. He is supposed to be paying the most attention. Obviously, my cousin was not doing that. Suddenly, out of nowhere, something told me to look back. When I did, all I saw was this dude driving his car right beside us pointing a gun directly at me with an "I got yo' ass" smile on his face. Just as I was about to yell out a warning, the guy pulled the trigger and I got hit in the mouth. The bullet went through my lip, then through my teeth and then through my tongue and came out on the opposite side. I was fortunate that I had a mouth full of gold and diamonds.

The guy lit the car up. He shot at us thirty-three times including the one that hit me in the mouth. I later found out that I had been shot with a nine-millimeter. My cousin immediately started shooting back. We got off the freeway and my cousin drove me to the hospital. I didn't have any form of bandages except for my coat so I held that to my face, in an attempt to stop the bleeding. The pain was intense.

Once in the emergency room, I had difficulty telling them what had happened to me, and that I had been shot. Blood was by now, everywhere. The security guard, who was inside the emergency room, finally understood what I was trying to say and ran to locate a doctor. I was placed on a gurney but refused to lay down, in spite of all of their efforts to get me to do so. They had no idea that each time I did, I was choking. The nurse was insistent so I reached into my mouth and took out the bullet and threw it at her.

During the course of all the commotion, I called my baby's mother, who eventually ended up understanding me enough and she called my mother. I was taken and prepped for surgery. The only thing I remember after that was a nurse standing over me and instructing me to count backward from one hundred. I made it to ninety-nine and was out cold.

I woke in a room at John Muir's Hospital. I saw that my mom was in the room. She eventually turned on the news and I found out that there were four shootings in Richmond that night. That was when I realized that the homies loved me for real. All of the shootings were done in retaliation for what had happened to me.

It took about three months before the swelling went down enough for me to be able to open my mouth. I was fortunate in that the bullet did not shatter my jaw, but it did fracture it. Even to this day, it has not completely healed.

EAST OAKLAND TIMES, LLC

The East Oakland Times, LLC (EOT) is a multi-media publication based in the San Francisco Bay Area. Founded by chief editor, Tio MacDonald, EOT has at its core three principles: the principle of the dignity of life, the principle of liberty, and the principle of tolerance. EOT supports the flourishing of civilization through the peace found by honoring these three stated principles.

Current Projects Include:

- Publishing of the My Crime Series
- The Publication of Original Inmate Art and Books
- Podcasts from California's Condemned Row
- Quarterly Print Publication for Free Distribution on the Streets of East Oakland
- Website Dedicated to Inmate Reporting on Current Events

Please remember by leaving a review you encourage others to buy the books in the My Crime series and thereby YOU support EOT's mission.

For exciting My Crime series bonus materials, such as original documents used for the composition of the book, go to www.crimebios.com

Support the EOT by purchasing EOT produced e-books, print

books, and audiobooks!

Stay positive & productive!

Unity in purpose!

Tio MacDonald
East Oakland Times
Chief Editor

EAST OAKLAND

www.ingramcontent.com/pod-product-compliance
Lightning Source LLC
Chambersburg PA
CBHW050600280326
41933CB00011B/1914